THE GLOW IN THE DARK BOOK OF OCEAN CREATURES

This edition published in 2003 by Frances Lincoln Limited,
4 Torriano Mews, Torriano Avenue, London NW5 2RZ

www.franceslincoln.com

Created and produced by Nicholas Harris and Claire Aston,
Orpheus Books Limited

Illustrated by Elisabetta Ferrero, Mariano Valsesia and
Gary Hincks

Consultant: Professor Peter Herring, Southampton
Oceanography Centre

British Library Cataloguing in Publication Data available on request

ISBN 0-7112-2254-1

Printed in China

1 3 5 7 9 8 6 4 2

THE GLOW IN THE DARK

BOOK OF

OCEAN

CREATURES

Nicholas Harris

illustrated by

Elisabetta Ferrero, Mariano Valsesia, Gary Hincks

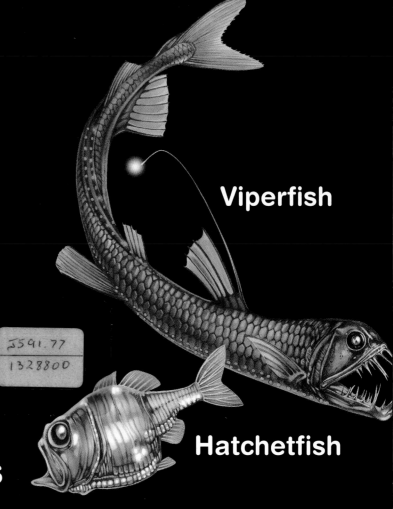

Viperfish

Hatchetfish

Firefly squid

CONTENTS

THE OCEANS cover more than two-thirds of the Earth's surface. They are home to thousands of different kinds of animal. Most live in the shallow coastal waters where there is plenty of food. A few ocean creatures live at greater depths, however. They feed on dead animals or plants that rain down from the waters above—or on each other. The deep oceans are cold and black. To see, or to lure their prey towards them, these deepwater animals create their own light. This is called bioluminescence.

This book also shows marine creatures that glow. For the pages with special glow-in-the-dark text and illustrations, look for the blue corner squares. Hold the book open at any one of these pages under a light for twenty seconds or so, then turn out the light. Have fun!

Gulper eel

ABOUT THIS BOOK

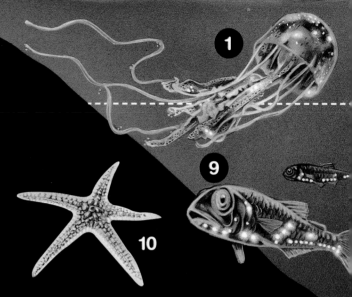

MOST ocean creatures live close to the water's surface. During the day, sunlight reaches down through the water. Here, tiny plants and animals, called plankton, provide a rich source of food. Below about 200 metres there is very little light. The few animals that live here must survive on dead plants and animals that sink down from above. Many deepwater animals are able to produce light from their own bodies. They glow in the dark!

1 Jellyfish
2 Black star-eater
3 Flashlight fish
4 Plankton
5 Hatchetfish
6 Black dragonfish
7 Shrimp
8 Loosejaw
9 Lanternfish
10 Starfish
11 Deepsea squid
12 Viperfish
13 Red comb jelly
14 Vampire squid
15 Deepsea anglerfish
16 Gulper eel

WHO GLOWS IN THE OCEAN DEPTHS?

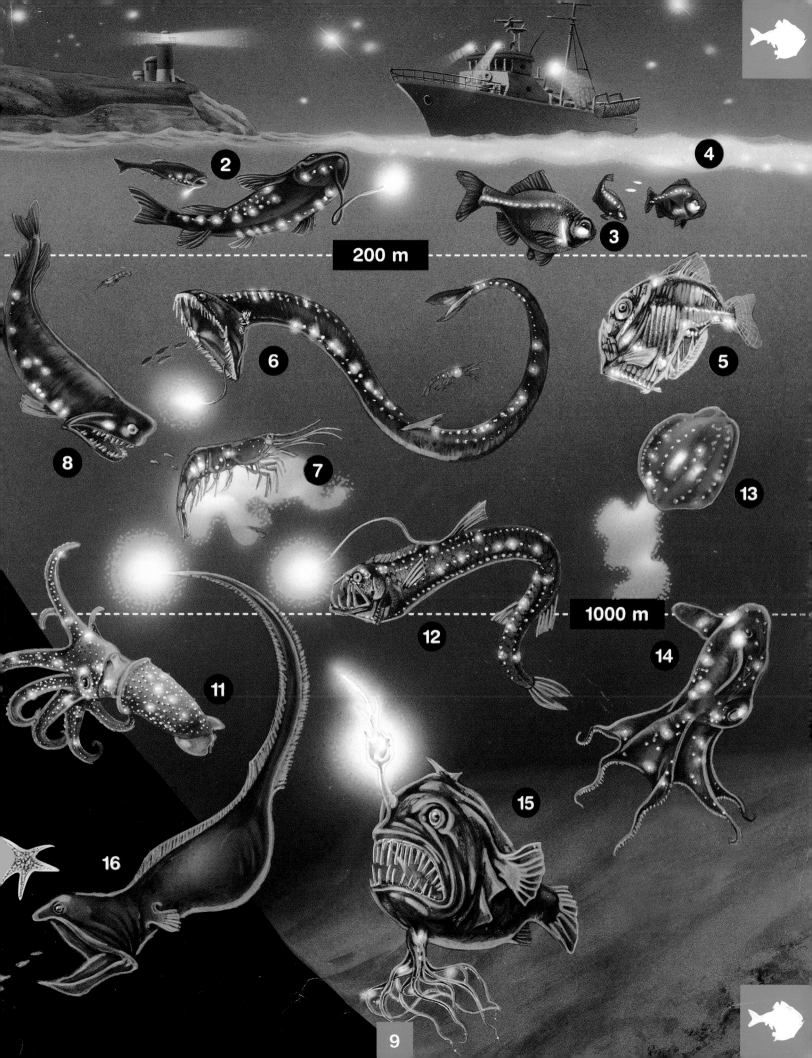

200 m

1000 m

9

CORAL grows in shallow tropical waters where it is warm all year round. Coral is made from the hard skeletons of tiny animals called polyps. When the polyps die, new ones grow on top of them. Over the years huge banks, called coral reefs are built up.

Coral comes in all shapes and colours. Many types of ocean animals live in nearby waters where there is always plenty of food.

LIFE ON A CORAL REEF

1 Angelfish
2 Marine turtle
3 Hammerhead shark
4 Kingfish
5 Butterflyfish
6 Parrotfish
7 Barracuda
8 Eagle ray
9 Moray eel
10 Starfish
11 Damselfish
12 Butterflyfish
13 Lionfish
14 Baler shell
15 Clownfish
16 Giant clam
17 Spiny lobster
18 Starfish
19 Seahorse
20 Nudibranch
21 Angelfish
22 Starfish

IN OCEAN waters more than 200 metres deep, very little light gets through. Only a few animals can live in the gloomy "twilight zone". Some, like the hatchetfish, the lanternfish and the siphonophore (a kind of jellyfish), travel up to the surface at night to feed. The viperfish lurks in the murky depths. It uses its long teeth to stab its prey. The light on its back fin lures prey towards it.

Siphonophore

Lanternfish

Loosejaw

CREATURES OF THE TWILIGHT ZONE

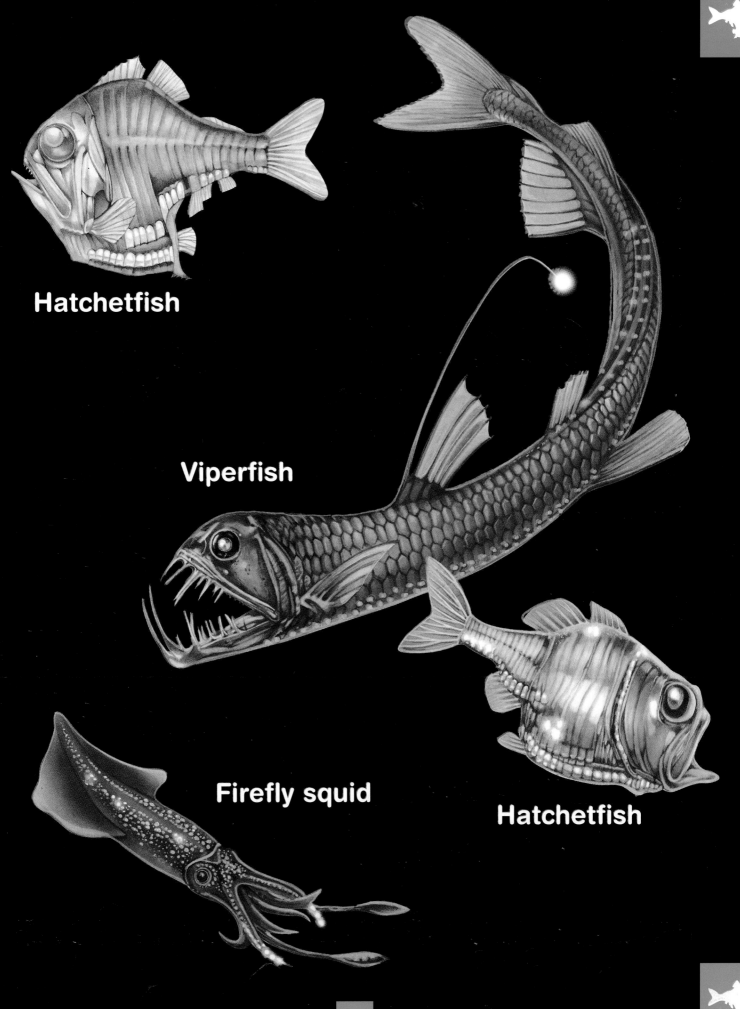

Hatchetfish

Viperfish

Firefly squid

Hatchetfish

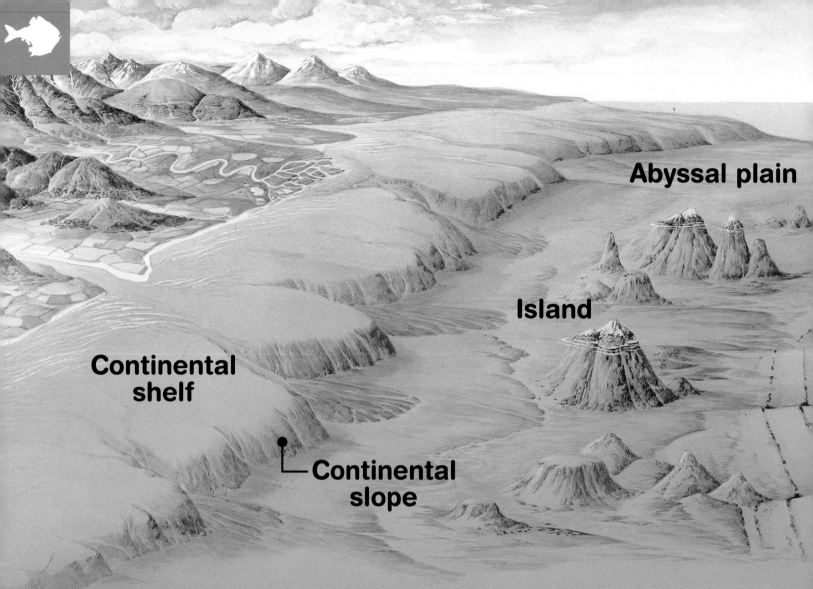

Abyssal plain

Island

Continental shelf

Continental slope

IF THE WATERS of the oceans were drained away, the ocean floor would look like this. Most of it is a level plain called the abyssal plain. Around its edges there is a ledge called the continental shelf. Here the ocean bed slopes gently away from the land, before plunging down the steep continental slope to the abyssal plain.

THE OCEAN FLOOR

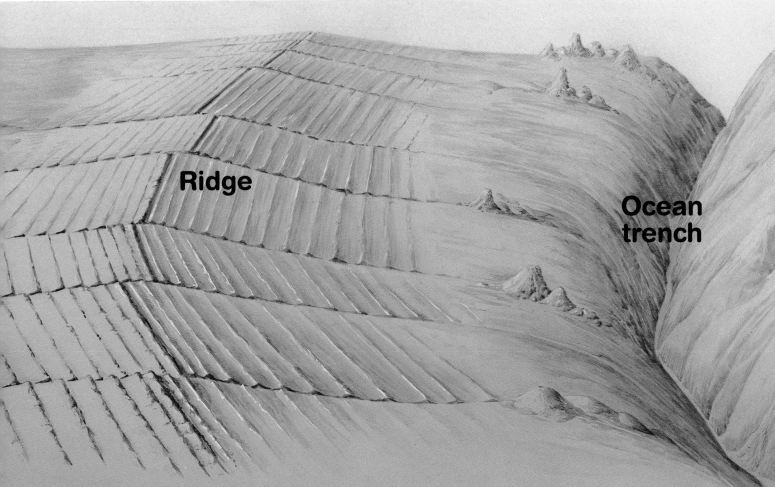

Ridge

Ocean trench

The abyssal plain is peppered with steep-sided mountains. Some of them are so high that they poke up above the ocean waters to form islands. In tropical waters, coral reefs grow up close to the shores of these islands.

A long, jagged ridge rises from the abyssal plain. Its slopes have long cracks in them. Also winding across the plain is a deep gash called an ocean trench. Some ocean trenches plunge to more than 10,000 metres below the ocean surface.

SOME animals live in very deep ocean waters, more than 1000 metres below the surface. No sunlight reaches these bitterly cold, still waters. But the water is aglow with light made by the animals themselves. The anglerfish and the gulper eels use their lights to catch small animals, drawn towards them by the glow. The vampire squid scares off its attackers by suddenly glowing.

Vampire squid

GLOWING MONSTERS OF THE DEEP

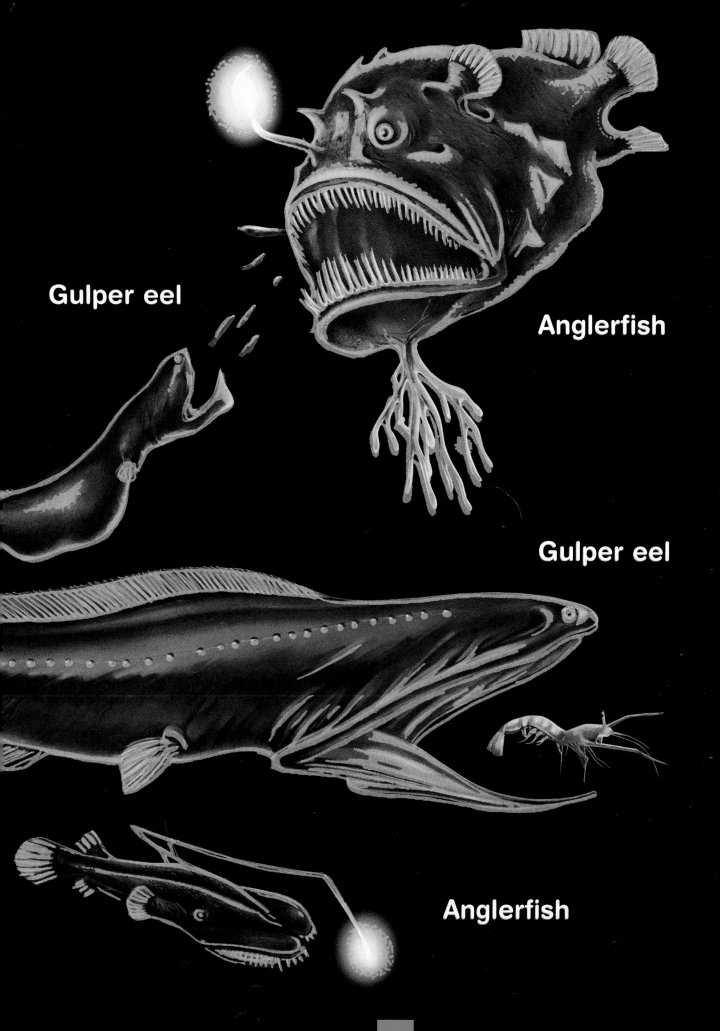

Gulper eel

Anglerfish

Gulper eel

Anglerfish

LIFE ON THE OCEAN FLOOR

WHAT LIVES on the deep ocean bed, thousands of metres below the surface? Here there is a vast, level plain of muddy "ooze". It is completely dark, icy cold and deathly quiet.

Some ocean floor animals burrow in the ooze. Sea pens stand in it like plants, while sea cucumbers and spiders creep about. Tripodfish perch on their fins and wait for their prey.

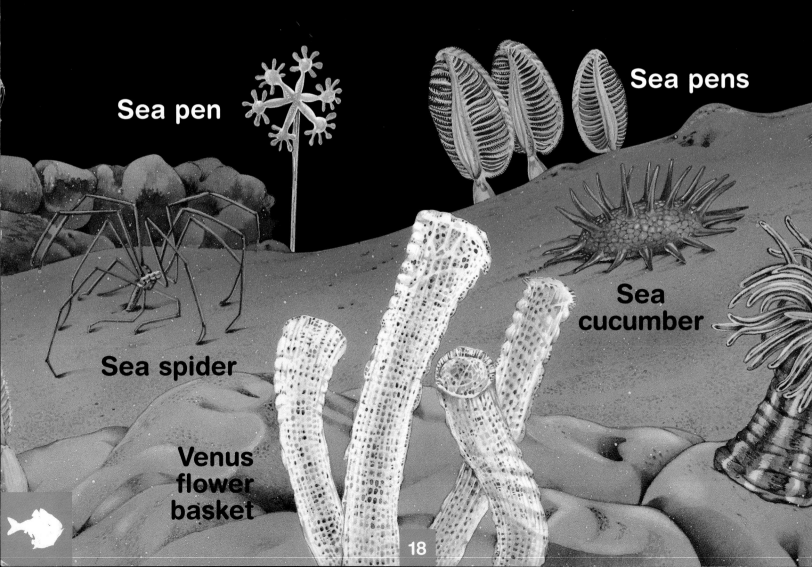

Sea pen

Sea pens

Sea cucumber

Sea spider

Venus flower basket

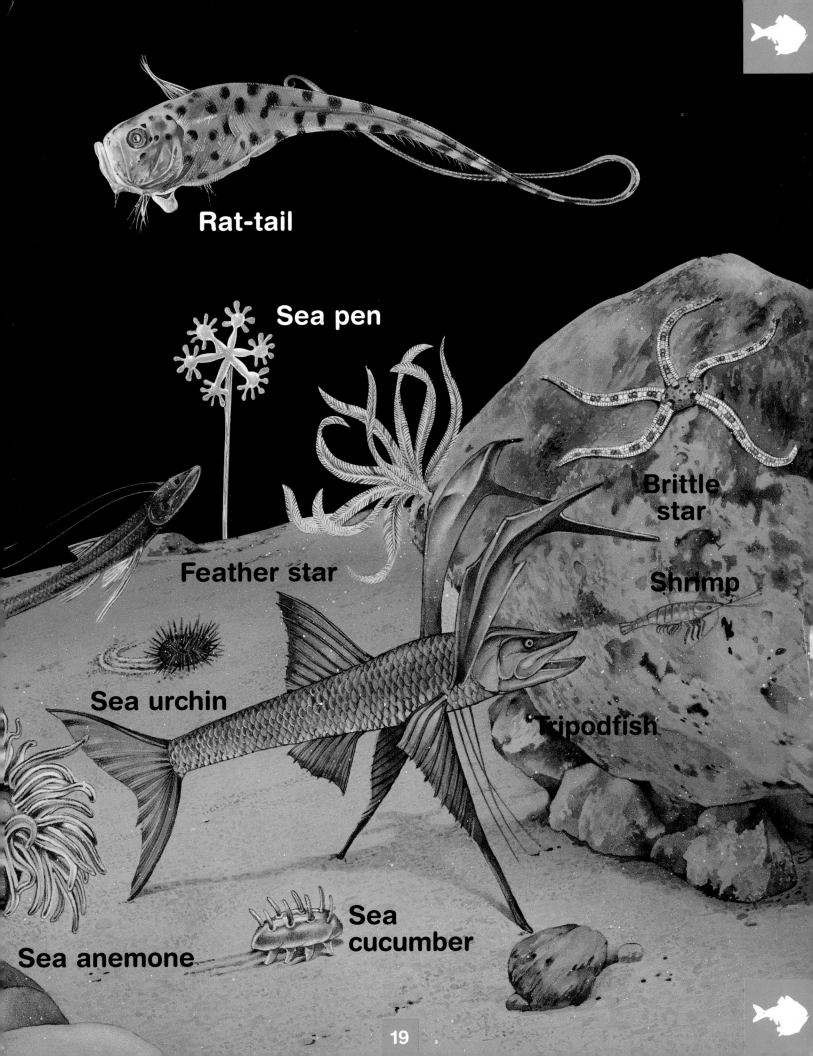

Rat-tail

Sea pen

Brittle star

Feather star

Shrimp

Sea urchin

Tripodfish

Sea anemone

Sea cucumber

OCEAN waters are brimming with microscopic animals and plants called plankton. Dinoflagellates are plants. They have no roots and drift in the water. We can see their detailed shapes through a microscope. Many produce light. Ocean waters sometimes sparkle with the light of millions of dinoflagellates. Copepods are tiny crustaceans, related to crabs and shrimps.

OCEAN MICRO-LIFE

**Copepod
(Gaussia Princeps)**
magnified 40 times

Dinoflagellate
(Noctiluca)
magnified 160 times

Dinoflagellate
(Pyrocystis)
magnified 160 times

Dinoflagellate
(Ceratocorys horrida)
magnified 1000 times

Dinoflagellate
(Ceratium)
magnified 700 times

THE SPERM WHALE can dive to depths of 1000 metres—and almost certainly deeper than that. It may spend up to two hours below water in search of its favourite prey, giant squid. No one has ever seen a sperm whale attack a giant squid, but it is probably a violent struggle.

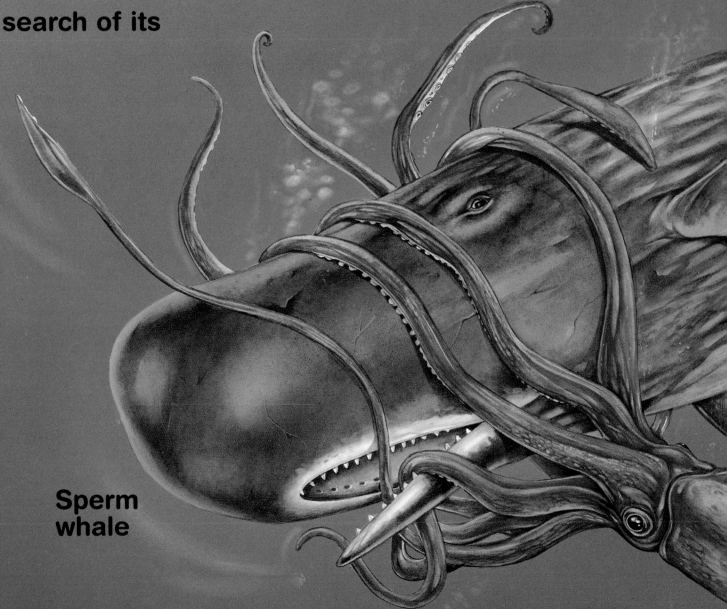

Sperm whale

SPERM WHALE, CHAMPION DIVER

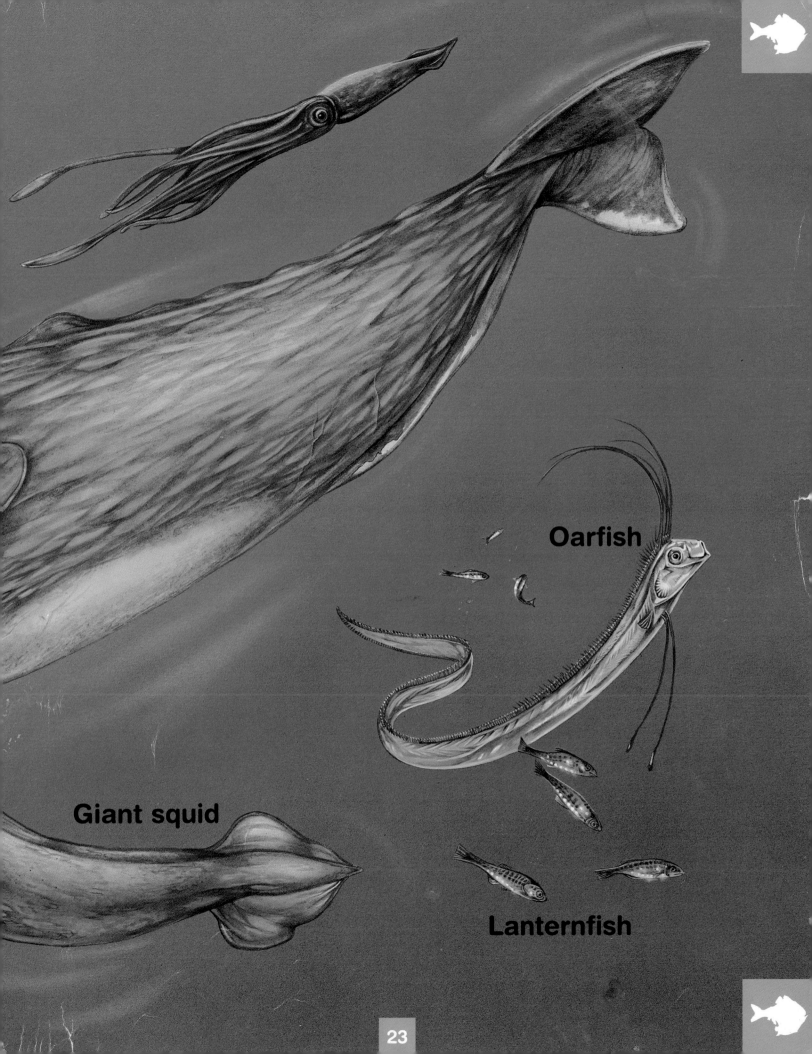

Oarfish

Giant squid

Lanternfish

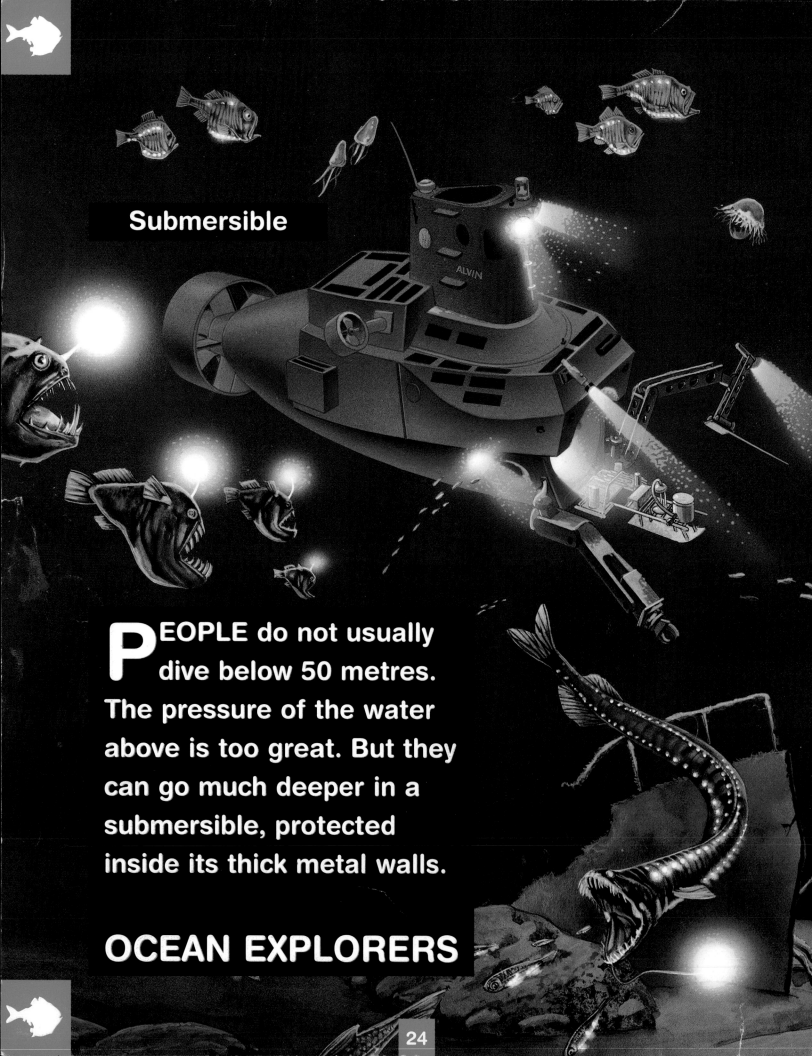

Submersible

PEOPLE do not usually dive below 50 metres. The pressure of the water above is too great. But they can go much deeper in a submersible, protected inside its thick metal walls.

OCEAN EXPLORERS

Using lights and cameras on board a submersible, divers can find out about wrecks and ocean life. Robots may also be used to take pictures and gather samples.

Robot

Shipwreck

Sea otter

OCEAN CREATURES are at risk from people. Modern fishing methods may lead to overfishing: too many fish are caught for their numbers to be kept up by reproduction. Whales and other animals are still hunted, even though they are protected by law. Pollution also kills ocean plants and animals.

Marine turtles, for example, are now rare. They have been hunted for their meat and shells. Sometimes they are caught in fishing nets. The waters where many live suffer from pollution. Some of the beaches where the turtles used to lay their eggs are now taken over for tourism.

Hawksbill turtle

OCEANS IN DANGER

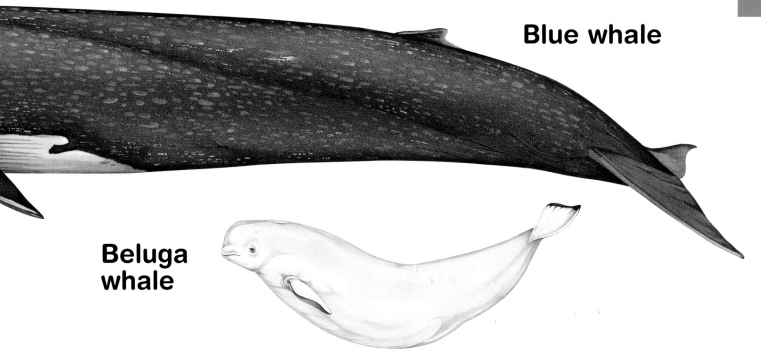

Blue whale

Beluga whale

This illustration *(below)* shows some of the ways in which the oceans have become polluted. Chemicals (1) sprayed on fields wash off into rivers then pass into the ocean. Waste is piped directly into the sea (2) or dumped from ships (3). Leaking oil tankers (4) kill many marine creatures. Old fishing nets (5) may trap dolphins and seals.

ABYSSAL PLAIN A large, flat area of the ocean floor. It lies between 4000 and 6000 metres below the ocean surface.

BATHYPELAGIC ZONE Ocean waters that lie at a depth of greater than about 1000 metres. No sunlight reaches here.

BIOLUMINESCENCE The production of light by living things. It enables ocean creatures *(above right)* to find one another in the dark waters for mating, or to lure prey.

CONTINENTAL SHELF Part of the ocean floor near the edge of the continents. It lies no deeper than 200 metres below the water's surface.

CORAL REEF A stony bank found in shallow, tropical seas. It is made by many thousands of tiny animals called polyps.

USEFUL WORDS

CRUSTACEANS Animals that have hard outer skeletons and jointed legs. They include crabs, lobsters and shrimps.

DINOFLAGELLATES Microscopic plants that drift on the surface of the water. Some glow in the dark.

OCEAN RIDGE A long mountain range that rises from the ocean floor.

OCEAN TRENCH A long, narrow, very deep valley in the ocean bed. It plunges to depths of between 6000 and 11,000 metres.

PLANKTON Tiny plants and animals that drift in the surface waters of the oceans. They provide food for many other ocean animals.

POLLUTION The spoiling of a natural environment by humans.

SUBMERSIBLE An underwater vessel *(below)* used to explore the ocean depths.

OCEAN FACTS

A sea is an area of salt water that is at least partly enclosed by land. An ocean is a vast area of salt water that lies between the continents.

There are four great oceans: in order of size, the Pacific, Atlantic, Indian and Arctic (some say there is a fifth ocean, the Southern, surrounding Antarctica). At 181 million square km, the Pacific covers about one third of the globe.

Why is the sea blue? Sunlight is made up of a range of different colours, called a spectrum. Blue light is scattered by seawater more easily than red, orange or yellow light. It is also absorbed ("swallowed up") more slowly.

The Arabian Gulf, where the waters are quite shallow, is the warmest sea. Temperatures may reach 36°C in summer. Waters may be near to 0°C at great depths even in tropical waters.

The tallest mountain (Mauna Kea, Hawaii, 10,205 m from base to summit), the deepest trench (Marianas Trench, Pacific Ocean, at one point 10,900 m deep) and the longest mountain range (the Mid-Oceanic Ridge, 65,000 km) are all found in the oceans.

The Great Barrier Reef, off northeastern Australia, is the largest natural feature on Earth. At 2027 km long, the reef is even visible from space.

The largest animal on Earth is the blue whale. It can reach up to 33 m in length. A baby blue is about 7 m long and as heavy as a hippopotamus.

The fastest creature in the ocean is probably the sailfish, which can reach speeds of over 100 km/h.

The box jellyfish is probably the most venomous creature on Earth. One touch of its stinging tentacles can kill a person in four minutes.

The largest fish is the whale shark, a gentle plankton-eating creature which can grow up to nearly 18 m long. The largest predatory fish is the great white shark, the largest of which may be up to 7 m long.